ANGER

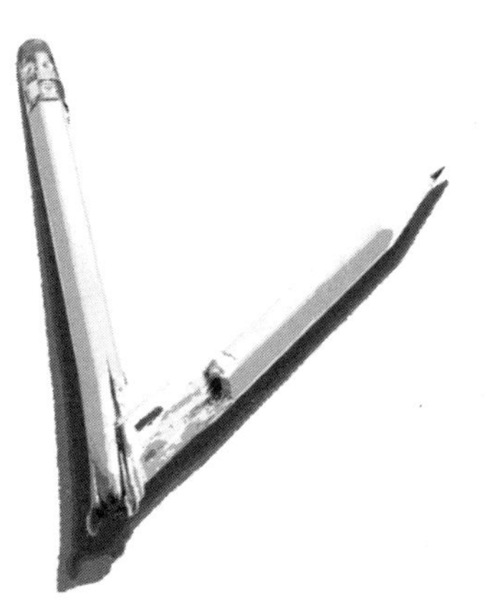

MINDING YOUR PASSION

ANGER

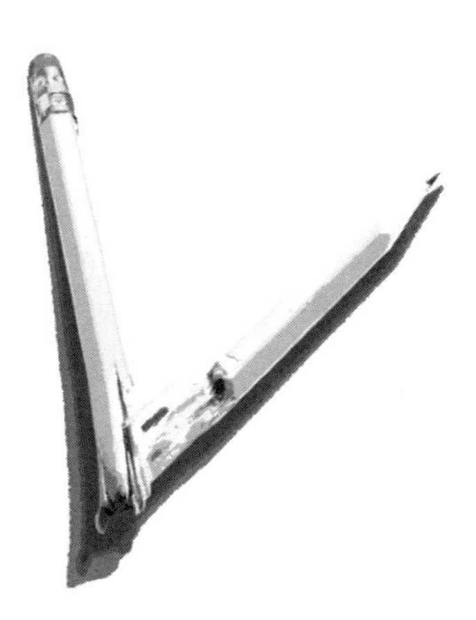

Compiled and introduced by

Amy Lyles Wilson

FRESH AIR BOOKS®
Nashville

For information, write: Fresh Air Books, 1908 Grand Avenue, Nashville, TN 37212.

Fresh Air Books Web site: http://www.freshairbooks.org

Cover design and illustration: Steve Barker, Canine Creative (www.canine-creative.com)

First printing: 2010

Pages 93–94 constitute an extension of this copyright page.

LIBRARY OF CONGRESS CATALOGING IN PUBLICATION

Anger: minding your passion / compiled and introduced by Amy Lyles Wilson.

p. cm.

ISBN: 978-1-935205-07-4

1. Anger—Religious aspects—Christianity. I. Wilson, Amy Lyles, 1961–

BV4627.A5A54 2010

241'.3—dc22 2009024286

Printed in the United States of America

Fresh Air Books is an imprint of Upper Room Books®.

Contents

INTRODUCTION

Amy Lyles Wilson

I was in my midtwenties before I ever had reason to be angry at God. Even then, I wasn't sure I could get away with it. In the small Methodist church in which I was reared, the preachers didn't advocate talking back to your Creator. Giving the Almighty the "what for" was not promoted from the pulpit. Instead, Mrs. Johnson taught me to make crosses out of elbow macaroni in vacation Bible school, and Reverend Marshall helped me memorize the Lord's Prayer. Mr. Cummings walked me through the New Testament, and the Trents chaperoned many a youth outing.

A wallflower during my high-school years, I did not know much about flirting and even less about dating. If you said I was not in touch with my feminine wiles, you would be polite. In actuality, I didn't even know I possessed such. Girlfriends I had. Dates to the prom, not so many.

So when, in graduate school, I met a good-looking, smart man about my age, a man who seemed to be as interested in me as I was in him, I fell hard. After several long conversations—the kind that make you a bit light-headed with surprise to find someone who thinks like you do—and a handful of promising dates, he found out he had stomach cancer. Rare in someone so young, his doctors told him, right before they estimated he had eight to twelve months to live.

They were right, and his funeral stands in my memory, some twenty years later, as one of the saddest afternoons of my life. I was despondent, and as is my usual response to something I don't understand or don't much care for, I went looking for answers, explanations, something. There was no bringing him back; I was rational enough to know that. But I didn't like it, and I needed to take it out on someone. It just did not occur to me that it could be God.

One source I turned to for insight was a favorite college professor, a Methodist minister who taught courses in religion and philosophy. When he told me I could be angry at God, I felt as if he were speaking a new language, one whose words I had not heard before. When he said to me, "God can take it," he might as well have been speaking to me in French, a course I had struggled with just down the hall from the very classroom where he had introduced me to Kant and Hegel, Augustine and Nouwen.

I have long been a hesitant kind of person, a worrier from way back. I admire from afar those people who claim to "act first, ask permission later." I have always been hungry for permission, to get the go-ahead from someone else. It has taken me quite some time to realize that I need only look inward for the allowances that matter.

Once my professor told me it was "okay," I practiced being angry at God. I was upset, yes, but I was also a product of a conservative, well-behaved upbringing. You didn't shout in my family; you did not go asking for trouble. Confrontation was not what the Wilsons of Jackson, Mississippi, were about. Instead, we tolerated what we could, put up with more than our fair share, turned the other cheek. So it took me a while to let God know how I really felt about the death of my friend. But eventually I was able to do it, to raise my voice and thrust my anguish heavenward. And it felt good.

The authors in this collection remind us that anger is natural, anger is human, and anger can be of God. It's what we do with it that matters.

FIRST THINGS FIRST

Thich Nhat Hanh

When someone says or does something that makes us angry, we suffer. We tend to say or do something back to make the other suffer, with the hope that we will suffer less. We think, "I want to punish you, I want to make you suffer because you have made me suffer. And when I see you suffer a lot, I will feel better."

Many of us are inclined to believe in such a childish practice. The fact is that when you make the other suffer, he will try to find relief by making you suffer more. The result is an escalation of suffering on both sides. Both of you need compassion and help. Neither of you needs punishment.

When you get angry, go back to yourself, and take very good care of your anger. And when someone makes you suffer, go back and take care of your suffering, your anger. Do not say or do anything. Whatever you say or do in a state of anger may cause more damage in your relationship.

Most of us don't do that. We don't want to go back to ourselves. We want to follow the other person in order to punish him or her.

If your house is on fire, the most urgent thing to do is to go back and try to put out the fire, not to run after the person you believe to be the arsonist. If you run after the person you suspect has burned your house, your house will burn down while you are chasing him or her. That is not wise. You must go back and put out the fire. So when you are angry, if you continue to interact with or argue with the other person, if you try to punish her, you are acting exactly like someone who runs after the arsonist while everything goes up in flames.

LETTING GO

L. Cecile Adams

I drove across a bridge that had been undergoing some repairs. Because of that, there was a place for me to pull off the road. I parked the car and surveyed the landscape. Suddenly, looking back across the bridge where I had been, I realized the scene matched an image that formed in my mind the week before during a meditation. The directive prompting the image was "Picture someone you are having difficulty with."

Immediately, a picture had surfaced of this spot and the person in an inner tube floating down the river away from me. I was startled, amazed, humbled, almost breathless, and almost afraid to move. My awareness of the previous week's image as a gift from God was heightened by the reality that I had never been in this place before.

My difficulty with this person had lasted long enough. I was angry about what the other person would not allow in our relationship and how the other person wanted me to live out the next part of my life. I had clarity that there was no returning to the way things were, and I was angry about that. I was angry, too, about having to go on alone—without the benefit of a relationship which had been significant for me.

I walked across the road and stood at the side of the bridge, looking down at the river which glistened in the sunlight. There was no other traffic on the highway. The only sounds were a gentle breeze, the calls of a few birds, and the music of the swiftly moving water. Standing there, I was able to release my struggle with the person who had caused difficulty in my life. In my mind's eye, I saw that person float on down the river, away from me and out of my sight. I felt immense relief and gratitude. Neither that person nor my anger were any longer burdens I carried.

ANGER

Frederick Buechner

Of the Seven Deadly Sins, anger is possibly the most fun. To lick your wounds, to smack your lips over grievances long past, to roll over your tongue the prospect of bitter confrontations still to come, to savor to the last toothsome morsel both the pain you are given and the pain you are giving back—in many ways it is a feast fit for a king. The chief drawback is that what you are wolfing down is yourself. The skeleton at the feast is you.

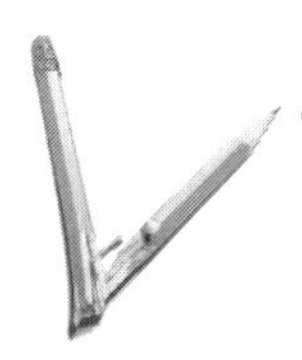

THE RESPONSIBILITY OF RAGE

Howard Thurman

For a long time there was current, as a part of the folklore of a certain section of the country, the story that during the month of August the rattlesnake sheds his old skin and a new one takes its place. There may be an actual basis for this in the life history of the snake. But be that as it may. The folk account is that, during this period, the snake remains immobile and is blind. At the slightest movement near him, he strikes out in his blindness, directing his attack by the sense of sound. If some object touches his body, in his panic, he strikes the spot that has been touched, releasing into his own body the deadly poison which he carries in his fangs. The result is death—suicide. In some aspects, this is indeed a telling analogy. A sense of defenselessness—fear mounting to panic—striking out blindly—destroying oneself thereby. The phrase "loss of temper" is one of those combinations of words descriptive of a total state of being. It means a dissipation of powers, a vital exhaustion. It is a blind striking at an object which often ends in deep injury, self-inflicted. Deep injury, because things are said, words are used, that can never be recalled or unuttered. How many times a man looks at the terrible work of his words, spoken in anger, and says, "I didn't really mean that; I lost my head." The injury to the other person is not the crucial matter here, important as that may be. For, after all, your words beat upon the outside of the other, and their damage of necessity is limited by that fact. The authentic damage is done to oneself. The dignity of the self has been outraged; a profound sense of shame and humiliation is present. This is no claim for repression and the complications resulting therefrom. But it is a recognition of the fact that to give oneself over to rage is self-destructive. There must be recognition of responsibility for one's action. A "loss of temper" is a luxury that carries with it a heavy tax that may send one into acute bankruptcy. It is in order to suggest that in the living of one's life, it is deadly to possess and encourage the mood that is expressed in the folklore concerning the behavior of the rattlesnake during the month of August. The best place for your temper is at home in you. There, it gives you power, courage, vitality; on the rampage, it is a terror—especially to you!

JUST AS I AM

Madeleine L'Engle

Cursing is a boomerang. If I will evil towards someone else, that evil becomes visible in me. It is an extreme way of being forensic, toward myself, as well as toward whoever outrages me. To avoid contaminating myself and everybody around me, I must work through the anger and the hurt feelings and the demands for absolute justice to a desire for healing. Healing for myself, and my anger, first, because until I am at least in the process of healing, I cannot heal; and then healing for those who have hurt or betrayed me, and those I have hurt and betrayed. . . .

Perhaps most difficult of all is learning to bless ourselves, just as we are. Before we can ask God to bless us, we must be able to accept ourselves as blessed—not perfect, not virtuous, not sinless—just blessed.

If we have to be perfect before we can know ourselves blessed, we will never ask for the transfiguring power of God's love, because of course we are unworthy. But we don't have to be worthy, we just have to acknowledge our need, to cry out, "Help me!" God will help us, even if it's in an unexpected and shocking way, by swooping down on us to wrestle with us. And in the midst of the wrestling we, too, will be able to cry out, "Bless me!"

I am certain that God will bless me, but I don't need to know how. When we think we know exactly how the one who made us is going to take care of us, we're apt to ignore the angel messengers sent us along the way.

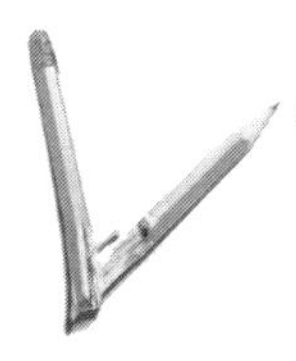

WHEN MEMORY SPEAKS

Renita J. Weems

I have flip-flopped over the years between being angry at God (the gods) for allowing my mother to abandon me and blaming myself for not being the kind of daughter a mother would want to stay and protect. But as always, in anger and in guilt the truth looks simple. But it is not. It is far more complex. It's as complex as knowing three decades later that God did not will my mother to walk out on her family and probably didn't try to change her mind. Leaving was her fate. Generations of abuse in her family and years of having no outlet to talk about it left her no choice as a frightened, defeated woman but to leave when the time came to decide. My mother left, and for good reasons I've discovered over the years. But to say that God didn't make my mother leave is not to say that God wasn't present in her leaving. God was present, like a weaver spinning a complex but fanciful pattern on her loom, offering her, me, and our family the possibility of healing and laughter beyond our pain. That's as close to what faith means to me as I can think of—that is, learning to make peace with all that has happened to me in the past, but especially what happened at thirteen, and trying to wrest from that past a blessing for me, my family, and those who look to me. Sometimes we think God is silent when in fact we are the ones who remain silent to God by our refusal to listen to what our memories are trying to tell us.

ACCEPTANCE

Garret Keizer

In times past the problem of the angry God was associated mainly with the tenderness of conscience. The guilty sinner winced at its force. Today that problem has increasingly come to be associated with the wounds of abuse. Victims of abuse have typically been victims of anger; for them the image of an angry God can be about as consoling as that of a black-and-blue Madonna. Thus, there are compelling reasons for describing a better path than that of the angry Father God on the wings of the storm. After all, probably every emotion we ascribe to God—with the possible exception of love—is a figure of speech. So we might do well to offer better figures, and to remind those wounded by abusive anger that God's wrath is partly, even mostly, figurative.

And yet there is a zeal for healing that kills. There is indeed such a thing as killing someone with kindness. The thoroughly gentle God, the unceasingly kind God, the God of the unalterable smile is also the fairy God, the clown God, the stuffed animal God—perhaps not a great deal more helpful than the threadbare little giraffe that a child clutches in his dark room as he winces with every cry from his battered mother's throat. The God who never gets mad for fear of offending the abused must sooner or later be construed as the God who never gets mad at the abuser.

Certainly that construction makes some sense within a Christian universe. God's love is not restricted to a certain class of sinner and withheld from another: God loves the abused and the abuser both. It can also be argued that what I have presented so slightingly as a "stuffed animal God" is none other than the Christ who suffers with and in every victim. But to divest God of wrath out of deference for those abused by anger is ultimately to salve their wounds with despair. It is to describe a God so benign as to be indifferent, so slow to anger that [God] is always late to save. It is to remember the Christ who suffered the little children to come to him, while we forget the Christ who said that their oppressors would be better off drowned with a millstone tied to their necks.

What is more, if we divest God of . . . anger but not of . . . righteousness, and if we continue to aspire to "be perfect as our heavenly Father is perfect," then we are compelled to proclaim that perfect righteousness for the oppressed consists of suffering passively without hope of recourse or retribution. We have heard that counsel before. Some would retort that we have indeed heard it before, and where we have heard it is in the Sermon on the Mount. Yet the most uncompromising practitioners of that sermon, Mahatma Gandhi and Martin Luther King Jr. among them, seemed to think differently. Gandhi, for example, eschewed the term *passive resistor*. Like King he saw nothing passive in nonviolent civil disobedience. The actions of Christ himself were hardly passive either. His cleansing of the temple was not even nonviolent.

Perhaps what the abused and oppressed require is not so much a change in metaphor as a change in identification. The wrath of God is not the wrath of the abusive parent or of power abused. It is the absolute claim of personhood asserting itself in the face of power and chaos alike. The voice that speaks from the burning bush says, "I have heard the cry of my people." The voice that speaks from the fire says, "I Am Who I Am." By implication we are who we are too. Our being is a value worthy of anger.

TAKE A BREATH

Gordon Peerman

As children are wont to do with their parents, my son, Alex, once instructed me in the uses of anger—when he was but three years old. A houseguest was staying with our family for several days, and my son, at their first encounter, engaged this man with openheartedness and the full range of his little boy enthusiasms. Our guest, a big, sturdy, sixty-year-old man, initially was charmed by the attentions of this small whirlwind around his feet, but during the second day of his stay, his response changed.

Alex's mother and I began to notice that our guest would correct Alex in what felt to us a heavy-handed fashion. He would engage Alex in physical "play" that was too rough even for this child who delighted in roughhousing. Our guest seemed to enjoy pushing Alex beyond the limits of fun into distress, then minimizing Alex's protest or upset by saying, "That's not hurting you." At this point, either my wife or I would intervene, breaking up the battle between the three-year-old and the sixty-year-old.

As the visit wore on, I got increasingly angry at the way our guest was attempting to control, correct, and intrude upon our son. Yet I was feeling stuck in the tension between wanting to protect Alex and wishing to avoid conflict with our guest. When our guest told us he had straightened out his own children with the back of his hand, we got the hint, and I responded with a cold silence.

Finally, things came to a head. Our guest was "teasing" Alex again, calling him a "rascal." There wasn't any humor in this name-calling, only an attempt to needle. I was about to intervene, ostensibly on Alex's behalf but also out of my own mounting resentment, when Alex took care of the matter himself. Drawing his small body up to his full forty inches, Alex got into his antagonist's face and angrily said, "My name isn't rascal! My name is Alex!"

There followed a moment of silence in which all present knew that the balance of power had shifted. Alex's mother and I exchanged a glance of a certain satisfaction. The teasing and the bullying stopped for the moment.

For Alex, anger was simply a part of life. Each night as he went to bed, his mother and I engaged in a three-question ritual, asking him, "What made you happy today? What made you sad? What made you angry?" He loved to ask both of us the same questions, and it was sometimes challenging to reply in a way that was truthful and comprehensible to him. He especially enjoyed asking us the last question, growling like a lion as he said the word *angr-r-r-y*.

Alex could hardly have known how much he was helping me by asking the question in such a playful way. Learning how to be with myself when I am angry at myself, how to be with others toward whom I feel anger, how to be with others who are angry with me—these struggles have been a growing edge for me for a number [of] years.

Both Jesus and the Buddha were models of nonviolence toward self and others, and they have much to teach about handling and caring for our anger. In Buddhist thought, mindfulness of feelings is the first step of dealing with anger, a process of *self-soothing* that gives us time and space to be with our anger before it becomes destructive. Christians have many models and examples for the next step in handling anger, *self-defining*, which stops demanding something from others and starts taking personal responsibility. The third step in handling conflict, *self-transcending*, takes us byond anger and blame and opens us to new possibilities in relating to others and to ourselves.

Self-soothing, self-defining, and self-transcending are the antithesis of the "get it out of your system" school for dealing with anger. As Father Thomas Keating points out in *Invitation to Love*, we need to recognize that our anger is our own, triggered but not created by another's actions. Anger often arises out of threats to our wishes for security, affection, or control. Life offers us regular challenges to these wishes, and unless we develop ways of holding the vulnerabilities underneath our anger in loving awareness, we will surely find ourselves controlled by anger when we feel threatened.

The well-known prayer of St. Francis of Assisi begins, "Lord, make us instruments of your peace. Where there is hatred, let us sow love." The prayer continues with a series of antitheses: where there is injury/let us sow pardon, where there is discord/union, doubt/faith, despair/hope, darkness/light, sadness/joy. If we read these antitheses in an either/or fashion, they would seem to suggest that our task as instruments of peace is not to feel or express hatred, doubt, despair, or sadness, but to suppress our feelings and enact their opposites. But if we read these antitheses in a both/and fashion, a different meaning emerges: the path to authentic love goes directly *through* hatred, the path to authentic union *through* discord, the path to ease *through* unease. This understanding suggests that the spiritual life is not an uprooting of our emotional unease but an attending to it so the kingdom of peace can be cultivated. This second understanding is truer to my own experience.

Practically speaking, I have found that suppressed anger has an unfortunate way of leaking out sideways in sarcasm, indirect expression through bodily tension and dis-ease, or direct explosion in aggression. My attempts to uproot negativity haven't worked. There is, however, a way of feeling and expressing irritation or frustration that goes beyond denial, surrender, or retaliation. This way employs not suppression but mindful attentiveness to anger, a willingness to wait and watch with anger until discerning what action, if any, to take.

This capacity for simple attentiveness to our anger is foundational to the skillful handling of emotions, for without mindfulness, we cannot begin to discern what to do with our anger or any other emotion. . . .

. . . This idea of caring for anger is very different from visiting it upon someone or hoarding it in bitterness. You start by simply noting the presence of anger. You don't make any attempt to tell the story of what brought about this mind state, but instead simply name your mind state with a soft mental note: this is anger. It's helpful to think of mental noting as a kind of mirror. When a figure (anger) appears before the mirror, the glass faithfully reflects the image without judging it in any way. Mental noting means letting go of analyzing in favor of just noting what is taking place.

This practice of mindfulness of feelings is the first step in caring for ourselves when we're caught in a storm of reactivity. By practicing this means of self-soothing, we can not only prevent the emotional storm from growing in intensity, but we open up the possibility of transforming anger into peace by giving ourselves time and space to embrace our anger.

A MOTIVATING FORCE

Sue Monk Kidd

Throughout this period of looking at Christian patriarchy for the first time, I felt deeply betrayed by a tradition I had served. I also became more aware of my anger.

In the beginning I'd felt the anger like a current, deep and distant, something molten and moving inexorably toward the surface. As it rose, I gave it few outlets. Except for a pen thrown across the room, an outburst in the taxicab, and a few other passing flashes, I'd kept a lid on it.

The church has been afraid of the power of anger. It has seemed to equate anger with sin. But was anger really sinful? What if the sin lies not in feeling the anger but in what one does with the feeling?

Most of my life I'd run from anger as something that good daughters and gracious ladies did not exhibit. Perhaps the thing most denied to women is anger. "Forbidden anger, women could find no voice in which publicly to complain; they took refuge in depression,"[1] writes Carolyn Heilbrun. Her words came true for me. Without the ability to allow or the means to adequately express the anger, I began to slide into periods of depression.

There were days that autumn when I had little energy to write or paint or even read. On days like that I felt like somebody had switched off the lights inside. Part of the darkness was the grief that happens when you realize what's been done to women and what we've allowed to be done to us. Part of it was because I didn't know where this journey was taking me and I was scared, and part of it was due to the loss I was starting to feel inside, the loss of feminine soul. But certainly a lot of it came because betrayal and anger sat in me like boulders and I couldn't move them.

I desperately needed to give myself full permission to get angry. The permission finally happened in a most unexpected way. I was having lunch with a young woman who'd recently been ordained as a minister and was on the staff of a large church. When I asked about her work, she told me about one of the first Sundays she had been allowed to conduct the worship. Before the service she had met the senior minister in his study. She was wearing a pair of medium-sized gold earrings along with her clerical robe. Noticing the earrings, the minister asked her to remove them.

"I don't think he wanted to call attention to my being a woman," she said.

As she reported the event, my anger suddenly issued forth in a stream of fury. Feelings of outrage and insult. Pure, unblemished wrath. I wasn't responding to that one incident, I realized later, but to all of the injustice done to women. I'd given myself permission to get mad as hell.

"Sorry," she said. "I didn't mean to cause you to get so angry."

"Don't be sorry," I said. "It's about time we all got angry at this stuff!"

The violation of women is an outrage, and anger is a clear and justifiable response to it.

As I released my anger more often and more consciously, the cycle of depression ended. I began to express the anger when my friend Betty and I got together and talked (she is good about letting me rant without interrupting). I pounded pillows. I poured the anger into my journals. I let it come.

Yet anger needs not only to be recognized and allowed; like the grief, it eventually needs to be transformed into an energy that serves compassion. Maybe one reason I had avoided my anger was that like a lot of people I had thought there were only two responses to anger: to deny it or to strike out thoughtlessly. But other responses are possible. We can allow anger's enormous energy to lead us to acts of resistance against patriarchy. Anger can fuel our ability to challenge, to defy injustice. It can lead to creative projects, constructive behavior, acts that work toward inclusion. In such ways anger becomes a dynamism of love.

Let's not look back in anger, or foward in fear,
but around in awareness.[1]

—James Thurber

❧

DEAR ENEMIES . . .

Marilyn Chandler McEntyre

You know who you are. You may think—because you're not holding me at gunpoint or blowing up my bus or seducing my husband or kidnapping my children—that I'm out gathering rosebuds for my suburban dinner table under the happy delusion that I have no enemies. After all, I'm a nice lady. People like me, by and large—some even admire me. And those who don't aren't doing much about it. But I do have enemies, and I know who you are.

You are the ones who hurt the people I love. You subject my children to propaganda and soul-sucking media manipulation. You try to make my husband and sons believe that masculinity is measured by willingness to kill and to make money. You drive my daughters toward self-destructive behaviors in the name of desirability. You poison the air, the soil, the water, the spirit, shorten their lives and damage their health for profit.

You are the ones who hurt the people I've been commanded and taught to care about. You drop bombs on innocent people. You vilify whole populations. Sometimes you torture them. You irradiate their crops and destroy their families. You drive them into debts they can't repay and call your usury "charity." You insulate yourselves from their pain, hide your atrocities behind political banners, and call that "virtue." You cover deceit with rhetoric, and exploitation with terms like "economic health."

You are the ones who set me at war with myself. You target my weaknesses and sins—my greed, my pride, my gluttony, my fear—and tempt me to measure my own worth by the satisfaction of my basest desires. So I eat too much, I work for public recognition, I buy what I do not need, I take my part in the racism and paranoia of our time.

You are the ones who take in vain the name of the Lord I love. You make a commodity of sacred words and images and a mockery of worship. You attack the Body of Christ from within and without. You are "them" and also "us," flying under both banners because your best strategy is confusion.

You lure and you lie and you threaten. You live in Washington and in the Middle East and Hollywood and in middle America and in my household and in my heart. And as the Psalmist says, you seek to take my life; you oppress me, surround me, and exult over me.

So when Jesus says "Love your enemies," does he mean you? And how shall I love you when you do evil? And why should I?

I believe that I must love you because we have been given to one another for that purpose. In some dark and mysterious way, we are gifts to one another. We have been given the historical moment, the circumstances, and the call to encounter in each other the very powers of darkness and light that afflict and heal this fallen world. And our assignment—yours and mine—lies in that encounter. We are here to learn how to love, how to exercise the power of love, even unto death, even toward those who violate what we hold dear.

I believe that I must love you because my life depends upon it. Not only the life of my body, but the life of my soul. Indeed, we seem to have no guarantee that the body won't be destroyed in the process of learning to love. But until I learn to love you, I am likely to remain in the squalor of my own self-righteous judgments, protecting my own point of view, condemning and cutting off some who may be the very strangers sent to give me a chance to offer the cup of cold water. I need to remember that the needy come clad in everything from rags to turbans to miniskirts to Armani suits. I need to remember that need sometimes looks like evil, and that it is perilous to judge too quickly which is which.

I believe that I must love you because I am like you. Every year I live teaches me the truth that nothing human is alien to me. When I was young, I thought Paul's claim to be "chief of sinners" was simply distasteful rhetorical posturing and false humility. Now I know that claim came out of a magnitude of self-knowledge, a self-knowledge worth praying for. So when I look at (and despise) your hypocrisy, your brutality, your greed, your self-serving propaganda, your abuse of power, your betrayal of innocence, I must open my mind and heart to that in me which is reflected in the mirror you provide. Perhaps it is latent rather than manifest. Perhaps its effects appear to be more innocuous. And yet how often the gospel teaches that we are in no position to judge what is small and what is large, and which is the mote and which is the beam. Comparing my evil with yours to reassure myself that I am among the righteous "misses the mark" completely—a term the Greeks used for sin. Counterintuitive though it may be, paradoxical, mysterious, and beyond all rational argument, your sin and my sin, your darkness and my darkness, merit the same condemnation and have been covered by the same amazing grace.

And so I believe that I must love you because you have been loved—lavishly, incomprehensibly—by the One who loved me, and who has put us into each other's hands to care for one another. Which makes me consider again, how do I love you?

I love you by embracing as fully as my imagination will allow the metaphor—and the fact—that we are brothers and sisters, children of one Father, imagined and willed into being by the same loving Creator. Whatever evil you do not only affects me, but finds some of its source in me, bound as we are in systems that perpetuate evil and in which we participate together. Your welfare is also mine, your shame is also mine, your struggle is also mine.

I love you by identifying the evils in which we find ourselves mired—the injustices, the brutalities, the deceptions, the greed—and holding them in the light. I love you by telling the truth as carefully and caringly as I can—about processes and effects, about who, in dehumanizing conditions, makes the clothing I wear, about what may account for the rage of the violent, about who is drinking the water polluted for our particular "benefit." I love you by holding you and myself accountable. I love you by not lying.

I love you by means of protest—speaking for—and by admonishment and by imagining alternatives to anger, war, unfair competition, and apathy. I love you by seeking out those who know something about how to love and have left us maps and means—the saints, the peacemakers, the earthkeepers, the ones who pray without ceasing. They have websites and retreat centers and flyers that hang in churches. They care for the widow and the orphan and also for the alcoholic and the people in penitentiaries. They love the woman agonizing about abortion and the one who had one. They visit Baghdad with bandages and also put on their ties and speak truth in boardrooms and on Capitol Hill. I love you by speaking and acting, against the evil you represent, for the life we are called to envision and live with one another.

I love you by learning to inhabit gray areas, by forfeiting the satisfactions of easy judgment and finding ways to sit down with you and find out what it is like to be you. I love you by studying your credo or your [sacred texts] or your party platform, your economic theories, your ideas of duty. And I love you by praying for the words and the wisdom to enter into the conversation that might redirect our energies into a path of mutual understanding.

I love you by praying for you, especially and precisely because you are those I experience as "persecutors." Jesus says to do this so that we may be children of our Father in heaven. What a rich and curious idea—that it is in learning to love you, my enemies, that I grow into my role and inheritance as a child of God; that in loving you I will deepen my relationship with the source of all Love. And in the process, perhaps, I will come to understand myself more humbly and fully.

I love you by turning the other cheek, and in doing that hard thing, learning also to discern the difference between self-destructive capitulation to evil and willingness to bear its cost for the sake of love. I love you best when I can follow Jesus' example in not returning evil for evil. Every time I resist the temptation to retaliate, I help prepare for the Kingdom in which I must hope that you are included, and that we will all be transformed.

It has helped me to remember for some years Germaine Greer's adage that "If the struggle is not joyous, it's the wrong struggle." She may not be a reliable theological touchstone, but I believe I can import that wisdom into my struggle to love you, my enemies. The struggle to love you is one in which joy is assured, not only as a final outcome, but along the way as a fruit of the Spirit that breathes and teaches love.

So how do I love you now? Badly. Intermittently. Sometimes grudgingly. But I know that we, you and I, are here to help one another work out our salvation, perhaps with fear and trembling. And so I must be grateful for you—not for the evil that you do, which is not mine to judge—but for the ways in which you, my enemies, are an occasion of grace.

MAKING ROOM

Flora Slosson Wuellner

If it is scary to name our hurt clearly, it is painful to let ourselves really feel the suffering from a past or present wound. To admit and feel emotional pain is to admit that we are not the invulnerable person we thought we were. We are woundable. Other people have the power to hurt us. To admit and feel this hurts us all over again.

Also we fear seeming weak and self-pitying to others. We may feel ashamed that we have not been able to put the pain behind us. We wonder if thinking about it, feeling our feelings, will make the pain worse or if we will get trapped in a prison of brooding. We worry lest our negative emotions endanger our health.

People around us, either because they want to help us or because they feel uncomfortable with our pain, may be telling us to hurry up and get over it. They urge us to look on the bright side and allow only positive feelings. This advice may be urged on us with the best intentions. Countless retreat leaders tell their retreatants to leave all their troubles and worries at the door when they come in. They lead participants in bodily exercises to shake out all negativity, teach them breathing routines to exhale all sorrow and anger. I know no quicker route to unhealthy forgiveness!

Making sacred space for genuine mourning over our wounds is essential within the journey of healthy forgiveness. Genuine mourning involves many feelings, including anger and sorrow, which are closely intertwined. One is often a disguise for the other. For example, if sorrow has settled into a long depression, we may have neglected to look at the genuine anger we are feeling. Or, if our anger grows out of hand and we unload it inappropriately on those around us, perhaps it is because we have not let ourselves cry. For some of us, it feels safer and easier to rage than to cry. Rage is often our masked tears. . . .

Some years ago I visited a church that was hundreds of years old. Our guide pointed out a crusted, blackened area in one of the old oak ceiling beams: "A slow fire began there," he told us, "deep inside that old wood. It smoldered unseen for many months, spreading slowly, creeping through the wood until it began to show on the outside. Then when it reached the air, it began to flame. We could hardly save the roof in time!"

We Christians are taught to be suspicious of anger, and many of us have felt that anger has no place within forgiveness. But anger serves as a warning signal that we sense a threat to something of value to us. . . .

. . . Continually shrugging off small, painful abuses and injuries as if they do not matter or as if *we* do not really matter is not healthy. If *we* become entrenched in the dangerous mind-set that Christians ought to go through the day as submissive victims, a dangerous buildup of unfaced anger can suddenly explode all over innocent bystanders.

THE GIFT OF ANGER

Ruth Woodliff-Stanley

Now and then, but not too often, I get really angry at one of the three members of my immediate family. Every now and then, one of them does something that makes me want to yell and cuss.

And, every now and then, *I do*.

And every now and then, one of them gets so angry at me that they want to yell at me. And every now and then, one of them does. I do appreciate the fact that, much as I may wish clergy cussing might surprise you, this is not entirely shocking news. At any rate . . .

Recently, I had such an episode with my teenage son, George. With his permission, let me tell you the gist of it. I was driving, and I was trying to work something out with him. He seemed to me to be disinterested in my words—not really present. It was a small but nevertheless nagging problem that I wanted to try to shift in our family routine. And I thought he was the key person who could change it by changing his actions. Well, after a while in the car, I blew it. I yelled . . . and I cussed.

Not the best behavior for a priest. Maybe I did it for shock value. Maybe I simply lost my temper. At any rate, it was an effective moment. Everything shifted. George and I went to a deeper place in our conversation. It seemed silly, in a way, but my overreaction, in that instance, opened a window to the place we needed to go together. I found out, among other things, that he was not at all disinterested. What appeared to me as disinterest was actually contemplation of something related to what I was saying. My probing led him into a long mental train that included a pretty detailed self-recrimination and self-evaluation, as it turns out. He was processing in a very contemplative way his own pain about the issues I was raising. But he wasn't able to say those things easily.

My anger unsettled him in his private contemplation enough to prompt him to tell me his thoughts. And I was able to tell him in a much more candid way the impact his actions were having on me. When I lost it, we both got more real and more present. In that moment, my anger was the catalyst each of us needed to come together, like a rather explosive but useful chemical reaction.

There are other times, mind you, when losing my temper is just that . . . losing my temper. And there is no redemption involved. And I will also note that whenever I do lose my temper, I believe a heartfelt apology is in order. It's not a good way to run a household—to go about losing one's temper all the time. Repetitive temper tantrums have diminishing returns and really wear on people. And it's also true that we have the greatest freedom to express our full range of emotions in our families. That can be both a blessing and a curse, but, when we use it well, I think it's mainly a blessing. To use it well, we have to understand its rightful place. Toxic anger is not what I'm talking about. Too much unfiltered anger can be harmful.

But there is something equally as deadly about being so afraid of our anger that we cannot express it when we are experiencing some sort of loss of connection from what matters most. Christianity has a side that is all light and love and peace, and it has a side that is profoundly challenging, like an unexpected outburst. And the challenge, I believe, exists to reconnect us to the most important things.

Danish theologian Søren Kierkegaard once said, "Remove from Christianity its ability to shock and it is altogether destroyed. It then becomes a tiny superficial thing, capable neither of inflicting deep wounds nor of healing them."[1]

There is a value to the anger we experience when what matters most to us is challenged. There is a story recounted in the Gospels about Jesus' use of his anger. John tells it this way: When Jesus saw opportunistic people taking advantage of the regular Temple goers through their monetary dealings, he fashioned a whip of cords, drove them out, and overturned their tables. When his disciples saw him, John notes, they were reminded of the psalmist's words about another prophet, "Zeal for your house will consume me."

The Greek word *zelos* comes from a root word that means "to boil with heat; to be hot." Our integrity is like a spark that blows off from the intense fire that burns within us. I'm talking about the fire of the passion for God placed within us at birth.

People may not know it or name it as such. But named or not, known or not, it is there, at least initially, for all of us. Over time, things threaten to bury it, to snuff it out, to leave it smoldering. It is a great tragedy when the human spirit loses this flame. When a person cannot find the flame, evil and despair have an opportune entry point.

The fact that Jesus got angry may not initially sound like good news, anymore than my outburst sounded like good news to George. But I believe it is good. It is a gift to see Jesus angry. It frees us, and it shows us that caring about something passionately, to the point of anger, can be deeply God-like.

Jesus is furious in the Temple. He is angry because the Temple is being cheapened. He sees not a fair market but an exploitative practice going on, and his passion for justice is ignited. When he drives out the money changers and turns over the tables, Jesus does something with shock value to bring home the importance of the integrity of the Temple—and ultimately, of course, the integrity of the people.

Jesus found the fire within, and he expressed it.

Anger exists to stoke the fires within us. That's its core purpose. When we use it to harm others, that's an abuse of its intent. Anger helps us avoid indifference. Indifference can impair our spiritual compass. Indifference is insidious. Over time, it can make us dull and ineffective.

You and I don't wake up and say, "I think I will become indifferent today." What usually happens is that somewhere along the way we get disappointed or injured, and we lose confidence that our actions can have any effect. And so, to protect ourselves, we learn to ignore our fire. We cover it with the cloak of indifference. At the crucial juncture, we tell ourselves, "Be quiet. Don't make waves. Don't speak your mind. Say your prayers and go home."

If we do this too many times, indifference gains a foothold, and life becomes deadly boring. And more importantly, God loses our voice in this world.

I'm not arguing for anger for anger's sake. God knows I'm not interested in a world filled with angry people.

As I said earlier, there are times for the useful expression of anger and passion. And yelling at each other in our friendships and communities, as I yelled at George, is not the best way forward, generally speaking. There must be very special conditions in place for people to give each other the space to yell—those conditions include safety and the right relationships for bearing the emotion.

What I am saying is that God is asking us all to *love* the fire within us. This is the fire that makes you truly alive. This is the fire breathed in all of us from creation.

This fire makes you want to dance and argue and laugh deep belly laughs. This is the fire that makes you believe this world can be healed and makes you work for it with all your might. This is the fire that leads you around a corner, just when you thought you had crossed every path there was to cross. The fire keeps you both bold and humble.

This is the fire that makes community worth the time and effort. This is the fire that gives life its purpose and glory.

My outbursts are sometimes holy, and other times not—as is the case, I suspect, with you. But through God's grace, I am learning in the course of a lifetime, to detect the difference. And I never want to lose the ability to care enough to get angry sometimes.

I am blessed with family who bring that same real presence to me. Since my exchange with George, guess what, the problem I was worried about is beginning to resolve itself. I think our encounter enabled us to touch the fires within.

Wherever we are called to go in life, we will not get there without the fire of God within us. We need to experience peace, joy, and love often in our most significant relationships. But that's not all. We also must experience zeal—the hot fire of God. Now and then, we need to be absolutely shocked—not just intellectually, but in our bodies, through our very senses. We need to be shocked enough to kindle the fire.

Without our fire, we will surely freeze to death. In its light, we will surely find the ardent love we desire. Let us be a people who stoke the fire. Let us be a safe haven from indifference.

The fire God places in us can burn hot. It is not a thing of comfort. But it is a thing of beauty and life and hope.

And so it *must* burn brilliantly and freely.

INSTEAD OF REVENGE

Kathleen Fischer

Baseball provides a lesson in redirecting vengeful feelings. Pitching coaches teach their pitchers that it really does not help to turn around and glare at a fielder who misses a play he or she should have made. Instead, it is much more effective to focus on the positive goal of striking out the next batter. Returning pain for pain does not work, but something else does. Instead of obsessing over a past hurt, we can redirect our energy toward the good things we want.

If we let revenge consume us, we will miss the songs of red-winged blackbirds, the colors of sunsets, and the laughter of friends. An ancient adage maintains that a life well lived is the best revenge. While attempting to strike back at another person proves futile, we have the power to create beauty and happiness for our families and ourselves. We cannot control another person's actions, but we can influence our own. Movement toward goodness balances the scale in a way that revenge never can.

Experiment with this idea for a moment. Notice how tight and constricted you become when you fantasize ways to punish someone who has wronged you. Then redirect your imaginings to gratitude for your blessings. Envision ways to bring about more of what you most value—health, friends, kindness, hope, success, love, community. Observe the peace and expanded energy this exercise brings. When anger toward someone who wronged you makes your sleep fitful and broken, try turning your mind and heart to prayers of gratitude. Begin by giving thanks for each good thing from that day; then move to the larger blessings of your life. When you refuse to pursue revenge and create less vengeful "movies of the mind," you still may experience pain at the injustice of life. Life's unfairness will continue to grate. You will know the price of refraining from retaliation. But you have begun to balance life's harsh realities with its goodness and blessings.

ANALYZING ANGER

Roberta C. Bondi

Fed up with the idealization of science and rationality, many of us have worked hard to learn to value our human emotions, especially strong emotions. We have found out the hard way that the man or woman who lives "rationally" at the expense of the heart is a wounded being who wounds others. We fear what we have been taught by popular psychology to call the repression of our feelings, and we want to welcome any strong emotion as proof that we are truly alive and untrammeled by a civilization that would have us deny who we are. We want to be full of a passion for life itself.

Our ancient monastic forebears are using the word "passion" in a different way. They would not speak of a passion for life. As a word, "passion" carries a negative meaning most of the time because for them a passion has as its chief characteristics the perversion of vision and the destruction of love. A passion may very well be a strong emotion, but it need not be. A passion can also be a state of mind, or even a habitual action. Anger is usually a passion, but sometimes forgetfulness is called a passion. Gossip and talking too much are also regularly called passions in this literature. Depression, the very opposite of a passion as we usually use that term in our modern world, is one of the most painful passions.

Strong emotions which accompany love, lead to love, or even are an expression of love are not passions. Real love, as opposed to manipulative love that serves the lover alone, produces more love rather than destroying love, and so it cannot be a passion. A strong desire to serve the poor will not be described as a passion in our literature. Mercy, hospitality, remorse so strong that it is accompanied by torrents of tears—none of these is called a "passion" because of their relationship to love. On the other hand, overreligiosity, scrupulousness about one's own righteousness to the point of seeing the neighbor as secondary to that righteousness, indifference to the well-being of others, a judgmental attitude—all these are "passions." . . .

Most of us are not done in by our great passions, by our towering rages, by hiding shoeboxes of money under the bed, or by our sneering contempt for the rest of the human race. The assumption in the early literature is that it is the little things we do over a long period of time that form character and make our relationships with ourselves, others, and God what they are. This is why some of what we read could appear to be nit-picking. Why does an Abba worry about his disciple picking up a dried pea that does not belong to him off the road? Not because a good monk is so scrupulous, but because the great and seemingly uncontrollable passions do not start out ready-made. They begin with small things that we tell ourselves do not matter: a general snappishness toward family members when we have had a hard day, a sense of self-satisfaction when someone we do not care for gets what is coming to them. This is where we all make mistakes. We are offended that someone should take a small act of inconsiderateness on our part as a sign of our lack of care for them, when, in fact, they are right. This is where our passions begin.

A MASCULINE PERSPECTIVE

Kent Ira Groff

Apathy is frozen rage.

—Mary, Chicago, 1969

Hope has two beautiful daughters: their names are anger and courage. Anger that things are the way they are. Courage to make them the way they ought to be.

—Saint Augustine

I will never forget the teaching of "Mary," who was brought from the streets of Westside Chicago at the time of riots in the late sixties to help teach us minister-types in a training program in urban ministry. "Apathy is frozen rage," she would say. Like a liturgical refrain, during this month-long seminar whenever someone described another incident of violence, we would hear it again, "Like I say, apathy's just frozen rage."

A couple of months later I took a course called "The Psychology of Education" at the University of Chicago from Allison Davis, author of a classic series on descendants of slaves, *The Eighth Generation*. . . . The course could be summarized by Davis's repeated phrase: "Depression is anger turned inward." . . .

Probably some [of my own] frozen anger lay behind my father's inability to express his feelings and his withdrawal from my brother and me in moments of need. Despite this habit of distancing himself, my father gave me two wonderful nonverbal gifts: tears and tenderness. I recall being held on his lap and feeling his unshaven morning whiskers against my face. And it may seem odd, but I can recall incidents that would trigger his easy tears, and I would feel close to him. . . .

What I did not want to admit to myself was a truth that I learned only in recent years from an addictions counselor: *When you see someone who cries easily, try to get the person to express anger; when you see someone who's easily angered, try to get the person to cry.*

When Augustine said, "Hope has two beautiful daughters: anger and courage," he expressed a transformative view of anger. One could also say, "Anger and tears are two gifted cousins."

I am sure my father's crying was related to painful emotions of grief. He told me how in his teen years he lost his father from a heart attack, how he quit school to manage the family farm, and how he watched as two different barns were struck by lightning and burned. Having learned from helping his father rebuild the first, he rebuilt the second with help from a few neighbors in the wake of his father's death.

Then there was the unnamed ghost in his father's family closet which he never talked about, but which my mother and a favorite aunt decided to confide in us when we got to be teenagers. I remember my mother taking my brother and me aside to tell us one summer afternoon. This "ghost" had caused my then-Mennonite grandfather Clarence Daniel Groff to be shunned by his community near Honey Brook, Pennsylvania: He had first married Kate Wanner, then later fell in love with her younger sister—and he divorced Kate to marry Sallie Wanner, my own grandmother. Fleeing to Haddonfield,

New Jersey, they were befriended by a Presbyterian layperson for whom my father was named—Francis David Winther. That is how my parents would later come to meet each other in a Presbyterian Church where my mother's father, Kent, was pastor. . . .

My mother and my aunt were the true heroines in this story. None of the men in my father's generation ever spoke of this secret. Yet because my mother opened this chapter of our family system, as an adult I have also been able to reclaim treasures from my grandparents' Anabaptist heritage.

Knowing the story has helped me think differently of my father. Had my grandfather still been a Mennonite when the two barns burned, there would have been instant community barn raisings, instead of long, laborious rebuildings. Had this thought ever occurred to my father or grandfather? There had to be deep, unspoken, unwept grief: "Give sorrow words. The grief that does not speak / Whispers the o'er-fraught heart and bids it break" (Shakespeare, *Macbeth*, IV.iii).

But just as this family pain was a source of my father's tears and tenderness, these have become his poor yet precious gift to me.

Somewhere along the journey I began to notice that I, too, cry more easily than most men, and I noticed that I was always trying to explain away my father's tears, at the same time explaining away my own.

In a macho society where "big boys don't cry," anger is a legitimate male emotion, but never grief. I can remember the feeling in my stomach when television cameras captured Senator Edmund Muskie crying in public, ending his political career. As Robert Bly pointed out in an interview with Bill Moyers, Abraham Lincoln was the last national figure to validate grief as a politically correct and healthy emotion.

Now I have quit trying to analyze my father's tears—but why am I writing about them? Just as I write these words, I am reminded of a TV program that reported how chemical analysis demonstrated that tears from deep emotions are quite different from tears from a pinched finger in the car door. The bottom line is that tears of anguish give the body a necessary catharsis. I trust this as good, down-home, spiritual, psychological, and physiological wisdom. A good cry is a good thing, a catharsis for buried anger and grief. . . .

Every man has within his life experience a hidden wholeness—as Thomas Merton named it, a metaphor of meaning, a healing hologram: this hidden seed, this secret leaven, this buried treasure, this mysterious pearl. But like the irritating grain of sand in the oyster, the place where it is buried is usually at the very point of anger, pain, and anguish.

As boys, we are taught that a wound is shameful, that to let a wound stop you from playing makes you a sissy. Yet Robert Bly's insight in *Iron John* embodies the radical gospel: "Our story gives a teaching diametrically opposite. It says that where a man's wound is, that is where his genius will likely be. . . . that is precisely the place for which we will give our major gift to the community."[1] While this especially applies to men, is it not true for everyone? Is this not the central meaning of Jesus' cross and resurrection? What is some life-in-death hologram that serves as a healing metaphor in your story-journey?

It was Jackie Robinson's mother painfully uprooting him from his abusive father and moving him to California that prepared him for his destiny as the first African American inducted into the Baseball Hall of Fame. It was Antoine de Saint-Exupéry's agony and anger in a forsaken New York apartment that gave birth to *The Little Prince*. . . .

There is no wound without pain, and no pain without anger. And that anger, whether buried or exploded, is what we must learn to pay attention to and to pray if we are to offer the whole self to God.

HOLY ANGER

Susan Gregg-Schroeder

Anger is an ongoing struggle for many of us. When I hear insensitive comments about depression, I get angry. I was, and still am, bombarded with comments such as "You've got so much going for you," "Look at the positive side of things," "Just snap out of it." And my favorite: "You should exercise."

While physical exercise often benefits persons suffering from depression, placing "shoulds" on a depressed person simply makes the person feel guilty, more depressed, and eventually more angry. I still find myself reacting too quickly, or even inappropriately, to people's insensitive comments. I began to identify triggers that touched internal, vulnerable places that I could not yet name.

Yet anger does not come as easily to me. I struggled while writing a sermon on the text of Jesus' overturning the tables of the money changers in the Temple. Because this story appears in all four Gospels, it is hard to ignore. Preparing my sermon, I realized that Jesus too had buttons that could be pushed. Seeing the busy, bustling scene in the Temple courtyard, Jesus suddenly was struck by the futility of all that activity. He was struck by the waste, the deception, and the manipulation for selfish human purposes. Maybe he saw the sickness in the religious institution and felt that he could not remain silent. He got mad and expressed that anger in very physical acts. This raw anger makes many of us squirm a bit.

Despite my preaching on this text, I struggled to express my "holy anger." I would get angry at someone, either from my childhood or present situations, and would be overcome with guilt for being angry. I would then get angry at myself and become convinced that the person with whom I was angry would reject or abandon me.

As a rule, the church has not been particularly helpful in teaching us how to express anger appropriately. Many of us feel guilty about our anger. We hear so many sermons on love, reconciliation, and forgiveness that we suppress our anger. I accepted the classical church teaching that equated anger with sin. After all, we've been taught that anger is one of the seven "deadly" sins. From the Sermon on the Mount in Matthew 5, we recall the words, "If you are angry with a brother or sister, you will be liable to judgment" (v. 22). The writer of Ephesians states, "Do not let the sun go down on your anger" (4:26) or "put away from you . . . all anger, . . . forgiving one another, as God in Christ has forgiven you" (4:31-32).

But we also cannot ignore scripture that confronts us with a God whose anger not only pervades the Hebrew Scriptures but enters the New Testament as well. The story of the money changers is a text where Jesus clearly expresses anger. To sidestep the issue of anger because it makes us feel uncomfortable is to ignore the fullness of the Word of God.

I must admit that I don't always embrace anger courageously. Often I push down my anger. Instead of directing my anger into constructive channels, I direct my anger toward myself. This misdirection results in increased feelings of worthlessness, in guilt, and even in suicidal ideations.

Like many people, I've learned to avoid confrontation by excusing others' behavior or by accepting the guilt or blame myself. Many of us have been taught to deny or repress anger; we want to please others. Women particularly evidence this desire to please.

Harriet Lerner has written a *New York Times* best-selling book about women and anger titled *The Dance of Anger*. She writes, "Most of us have received little help in learning to use our anger to clarify and strengthen ourselves and our relationships. Instead, our lessons have encouraged us to fear anger excessively, to deny it entirely, to displace it onto inappropriate targets, or to turn it against ourselves."[1]

Through many societal and church teachings, I've internalized the belief that anger is unacceptable. It is the opposite of forgiveness and is, therefore, a nonspiritual reaction. But I am learning that anger is an important aspect of our spiritual journey and that healthy anger can be holy anger. It is not what we feel that is sinful; it is what we do with our feelings. Holy, righteous anger can serve as a powerful catalyst for change. We in the church can transform anger into energy for love by providing available avenues for the expression of anger in healthy ways.

Flora Slosson Wuellner is a retreat leader, spiritual guide, and ordained minister in the United Church of Christ. Her book *Heart of Healing, Heart of Light* has helped me learn to deal with my anger. Reverend Wuellner talks about two major forms of anger. The first she calls "infected anger." Infected anger is murky and unclear; we aren't really sure at whom or at what we are angry. We just know that we are angry. Often something quite minor can trigger infected anger, and we explode or lash out in a destructive way. Infected anger may be individual or communal, and persons may easily manipulate this anger to target certain individuals or groups.

Reverend Wuellner calls the other kind of anger "clear" anger. She describes it as "the clean, healthy flame of outraged justice and humanity."[2] This anger has a cause, a reason that we know and acknowledge. She states,

> This anger can be a powerful, creative energy for defiance of evil, for decision making, for protection of self and others, and for limit-setting. It is out of this clear anger that forgiveness and reconciliation from healthy roots can eventually rise.[3]

I am coming to understand that facing anger and being open to its transforming and healing power is part of my spiritual journey. Clear anger calls us to confront and stop abuse and injustice of all kinds, as Jesus did.

Clear anger, or what I call holy anger, can communicate with and even convert others toward a vision of God's kingdom. Holy anger can unite us in a common purpose. . . . Slowly I am learning to embrace anger as a God-given emotion, both individually and collectively. Anger is an emotional energy deep within us that signals a warning that all is not right. Anger demands a change of some sort. Thus, anger has the power to move us enough so that we disrupt the status quo and challenge the injustice or wrong that touches us so deeply. It takes tremendous courage to embrace such a powerful emotion, but the courage comes when we truly believe that anger is God's gift.

THE ART OF ESSENTIAL FRUSTRATION

Karla M. Kincannon

Every time an artist begins a new project, confusion and chaos are built into it. The resulting frustration, this natural ingredient of creativity, comes from sorting through numerous possibilities for the best solution to the current creative challenge. It acts as the grain of sand in the oyster from which the pearl of an idea manifests. Though frequently less than fun, without frustration, there would be no art.

No matter how many creative projects I undertake, the frustration stage still takes me by surprise. I erroneously expect creativity to be smooth and effortless. Associating frustration with lack of talent, I tell myself, *If I were really gifted I wouldn't feel this frustrated.* This faulty reasoning resembles the spiritual pilgrim's mistaken belief that *good Christians never get angry or feel upset by the challenges of life.* Nonsense! Emotions—for the artist and the spiritual pilgrim—simply come with being human. They have nothing to do with how much talent we have or how faithful we are. Emotions provide grist for the mill, tools for your growth. The problem develops when an emotion overtakes us, and we get stuck in it. Each time I come to this phase of the creative process, I am tempted, if only briefly, to give up. I want to run from frustration like Jonah ran from Nineveh—full speed in the opposite direction. However, I cannot escape my call. I can stall the creative process for a while and frequently do. I hide out by pretending the project has no importance for me. Other legitimate needs in my life take on exaggerated urgency. Usually it is not the trivial things that stall the process but good and well-intentioned stuff—like my mission the day after our dog encountered a skunk.

We were expecting a houseguest one evening when I was feeling frustrated with a writing project. All the ideas and words in my head seemed jumbled in one chaotic mess. Nothing I wrote made sense. It suddenly became imperative that I remove the faint but lingering traces of skunk scent off the dog and out of the guest bathtub where my dutiful spouse had bathed the dog numerous times. My husband had scoured the tub in an attempt to eliminate the odor, but the scent of skunk hung on. Like a Stepford wife, I found myself scrubbing the bathtub at four different intervals on the day we expected the houseguest. I interspersed the cleaning with Internet research on removal of skunk odor. While a clean-smelling bathroom is more hospitable than one that smells bad, it is also true that we had another bathroom available for guests. The more frustrated I became with my writing, the more critical it became to have a bathtub free from the almost-imperceptible traces of skunk odor.

The frustration at this stage of the creative process causes many artists to abandon creativity altogether in order to avoid the discomfort accompanying this phase. The painting remains undone because emotions get in the way; agitation keeps the great ideas and good intentions from ever coming to fruition. I know an artist who gets all excited over an idea for a new project, seems to proceed at a rapid pace, then runs up against the brick wall of frustration at full speed. That stops him cold. The expectation that creativity should always feel good and be easy is his brick wall. His creative idea dies on impact and so does a little of his artist's spirit, especially since his pattern recurs. If he ever wants to complete a project, he must learn to deal with the frustration that makes him want to throw paint on the wall instead of applying it to canvas.

Forcing a premature conclusion to the creative process also tempts the artist who dislikes frustration. Watching a friend create, I am struck by how her process develops. Her prototype looks good enough to sell; but by going deeper into her creativity, she ends up with a masterpiece. The prototype now looks like a shadow of the complete work. Sometimes in my work, I'd like to settle for the prototype just so I will not have to plumb the depths of the creative process. Getting to the marrow of the initial inspiration requires hard and lonely work. But, like a person committed to a cause, I press on because to force a premature conclusion to the creative process fails to let the work of art be all it can be.

When tempted to run like Jonah, I remind myself that frustration is not just a stage to endure, although sometimes a tenacious endurance may be our best effort. As childbirth requires labor pains, creativity necessitates frustration as part of the process. It causes the artist to go deeper into the source of creativity, bringing forth new life and energy previously known only in the imagination. Once the labor pains of creativity have begun, the only way out of the frustration—without aborting the creative idea—leads straight through it. Out of chaos comes brilliance and beauty if the artist will stay with the process.

SUGGESTIONS FOR HANDLING ANGER IN YOUR LIFE

1

Acknowledge your anger.

2

Weigh it. Is it worth your time and energy to be reactionary?

3

Volunteer with an organization that puts you in direct contact with people. Find out which groups serve which populations in your community and match your interests and talents with their needs.

4

Seek professional help if you can't deal with your anger on your own.

5

Don't let your anger simmer. The longer you ignore it—or pretend it doesn't exist—the more destructive its potential.

6

Consider that the person who has angered you may not even be aware that he or she has hurt you.

7

Make room for forgiveness.

8

Don't take out your anger on your loved ones, or yourself.

9

Develop a ritual for letting go of your anger. Write down your feelings about the offense and then burn the piece of paper or put it in a shredder as a symbol of release.

10

Go ahead, let God know how you feel. God can take it.

A Motivating Force

1. Carolyn G. Heilbrun, *Writing a Woman's Life* (New York: Ballantine Books, 1988), 15.

Let's Not Look Back

1. James Thurber, foreword to *Lanterns and Lances* (New York: Harper and Brothers, 1961), xv.

The Gift of Anger

1. Søren Kierkegaard as quoted by Joe Ross in "The Foolishness of the Cross," *Sojourners*, August 2007.

A Masculine Perspective

1. Robert Bly, *Iron John: A Book about Men* (Reading, MA: Addison-Wesley, 1990), 42.

Holy Anger

1. Harriet Goldhor Lerner, *The Dance of Anger* (New York: Harper and Row, 1986), 10.
2. Flora Slosson Wuellner, *Heart of Healing, Heart of Light* (Nashville, TN: Upper Room Books, 1992), 73.
3. Ibid.

Contributors

L. Cecile Adams is Chief Creative Coach at the Creative Coaching Center, coaching people to joyful living.

Roberta C. Bondi, Ph.D., retired from the Candler School of Theology at Emory University in 2006.

Frederick Buechner, an ordained Presbyterian minister, is the author of more than thirty books. He has been a finalist for the National Book Award and the Pulitzer Prize.

Kathleen Fischer works as a psychotherapist and spiritual director in Seattle. Dr. Fisher is the author of several books, including *Winter Grace: Spirituality and Aging* and *Women at the Well: Feminist Perspectives on Spiritual Direction.*

Susan Gregg-Schroeder founded Mental Health Ministries to provide educational resources to help erase the stigma of mental illness in our faith communities. She shares her personal story as she struggled with severe depression in her book, *In the Shadow of God's Wings: Grace in the Midst of Depression.*

Kent Ira Groff is a writer and retreat director living in Colorado. His books include *Active Spirituality: A Spiritual Guide for Seekers and Ministers* and *Journeymen: A Spiritual Guide for Men.*

Thich Nhat Hanh is an expatriate Vietnamese Zen Buddhist monk, teacher, author, poet, and peace activist. He has published more than one hundred books.

Garret Keizer has written numerous critically acclaimed books, including *Help: The Original Human Dilemma*, *The Enigma of Anger*, and *A Dresser of Sycamore Trees*. He is a regular contributor to *Harper's Magazine* and *The Christian Century.*

Sue Monk Kidd is the author of *When the Heart Waits* and *The Dance of the Dissident Daughter*, among others. Her two novels, *The Secret Life of Bees* and *The Mermaid Chair*, spent time on the *New York Times* best-seller list.

Karla M. Kincannon, an artist and United Methodist minister, founded SpiritArt Ministries, an innovative spiritual direction practice. She is also a lecturer, teacher, and retreat leader.

Madeleine L'Engle (1918–2007) wrote more than sixty books.

Marilyn Chandler McEntyre is a Fellow at the Gaede Institute for the Liberal Arts, Westmont College, Santa Barbara, California.

Gordon Peerman is a psychotherapist and consultant. An Episcopal priest, he holds degrees from the University of Virginia, Yale, and Vanderbilt, and has taught at Vanderbilt University Divinity School.

James Thurber (1894–1961), a humorist and cartoonist, was widely known for his work with *The New Yorker*.

Howard Thurman (1899–1981) was a graduate of Morehouse College and Colgate-Rochester Theological Seminary. He served on the faculty of Howard University as Professor of Theology and Dean of Rankin Chapel, and was Dean of Marsh Chapel at Boston University.

Renita J. Weems, Ph.D., is a minister, teacher, and writer. Her book *Listening for God: A Minister's Journey through Silence and Doubt* won the Religious Communicators' Council's 1999 Wilbur Award for excellence in communicating spiritual values to the secular media.

Amy Lyles Wilson is a writer in Nashville, Tennessee, who received a master's degree from Vanderbilt University Divinity School. Her work has appeared on National Public Radio, and she is a columnist for *Her Nashville* magazine. (www.amylyleswilson.com.)

Ruth Woodliff-Stanley is an Episcopal priest and licensed clinical social worker in Denver, Colorado. She is priest-in-charge of St. Thomas and helps churches and other groups address conflict and transition.

Flora Slosson Wuellner is a teacher, retreat leader, spiritual director, and ordained minister in the United Church of Christ.

The following pages constitute an extension of the copyright page.

The articles in this book are reprinted with permission. The publisher gratefully acknowledges the following:

L. Cecile Adams, "Along the River to Release," *Alive Now* (January/February 2001):50–51.

Excerpt from TO LOVE AS GOD LOVES by Roberta C. Bondi, copyright © 1987 Fortress Press. Used by permission of Augsburg Fortress.

"Anger" from WISHFUL THINKING: A THEOLOGICAL ABC by FREDERICK BUECHNER. Copyright © 1973 by Frederick Buechner. Reprinted by permission of HarperCollins Publishers.

Excerpt from Kathleen Fischer, F*orgiving Your Family: A Journey to Healing* © Copyright 2005 by Kathleen Fischer. Used by permission of Upper Room Books. All rights reserved.

Excerpt from Susan Gregg-Schroeder, *In the Shadow of God's Wings: Grace in the Midst of Depression* © 1997 by Susan Gregg-Schroeder. Used by permission of Upper Room Books. All rights reserved.

Excerpt from Kent Ira Groff, *Journeymen: A Spiritual Guide for Men (and for Women Who Want to Understand Them)* © 1999 by Kent Ira Groff. Used by permission of Upper Room Books. All rights reserved.

"Putting Out the Fire of Anger," from ANGER by Thich Nhat Hanh, copyright © 2001 by Thich Nhat Hanh. Used by permission of Riverhead Books, an imprint of Penguin Group (USA) Inc.

Excerpt from Garret Keizer, *The Enigma of Anger: Essays on a Sometimes Deadly Sin*, copyright © 2002 by Garret Keizer. Reprinted with permission of John Wiley & Sons, Inc.

Excerpt from pp. 73–75 from THE DANCE OF THE DISSIDENT DAUGHTER by SUE MONK KIDD. Copyright © 1996 by Sue Monk Kidd. Reprinted by permission of HarperCollins Publishers.